# I'm Too Dumb
## to Be Friends With

by

## Steve Cohen

DORRANCE
PUBLISHING CO
EST. 1920
PITTSBURGH, PENNSYLVANIA 15238

Dorrance Publishing Co
585 Alpha Drive
Pittsburgh, PA 15238
Visit our website at *www.dorrancebookstore.com*

ISBN: 978-1-6366-1390-1
eISBN: 978-1-6366-1967-5

*This book is dedicated to my father,*
*Dr. Mark E Cohen, PhD,*
*the smartest person I've ever known*

# Contents

# Foreword

*I* am going to spoil this book at the outset, right here, right now... I am a forty-eight-year-old man and I know that I AM DUMB. These next chapters will only go to prove this conclusion.

I didn't always consider myself dumb, though. Once upon a time, I considered myself pretty smart. Actually, I considered myself very intelligent and even brilliant. That was from 1979-1981. During those years, I knew all answers, made no poor choices, and was measurably more intelligent than my peers. Those years were first and second grade. Everything was easy to me during that time. I would go to class and everything was easy as pie. There was nothing my teacher could ask me to which I wouldn't confidently raise my hand and provide the perfect answer. I was well behaved, knew how to add and subtract... RAPIDLY I might add, I was in the BLUE reading group... the absolute highest! And my handwriting was so exemplary that you would want to frame my papers and hang them on your wall. I was the teacher's pet and she let me know how great I was. And she'd call my parents and share my achievements, natural skill, and brilliance. And in turn, my parents would praise me and tell me how smart I was. Looking back, I really was amazing. That was my first clue that my brain may be one for the ages. But then I got the proof!

In second grade, my entire class was given the CATs. The California Achievement Tests. We spent an entire week answering multiple-choice questions and filling in circles with our No. 2 pencils, and I loved it. The answers just kept coming to me and I was a bubble-filling machine. C, A, A, D, C, B, B, A, and on and on and on I'd go, eventually completing the tests well before my peers. My poor eight-year-old peers.

Sure enough, a couple weeks later, when my parents got the results of my CATs, we got documented proof of my geniusness. I was in the 99th percentile in EVERY category (100 percent wasn't a possibility). I was the smartest in my class AND POSSIBLY IN THE WORLD! My parents knew it, my teachers knew it, and now I knew it.

After second grade, life started getting more challenging. I often didn't rise to that challenge and didn't show the same levels of brain power as I did between '79–'81, but the conclusion that I was a genius stuck with me. For a long time, through my teens, twenties, and thirties. Not that things were easy to me for all those years. They certainly were not. Just during those years, I would blame other things for my incorrect answers, poor choices, and errors. I'd blame bad luck. Blame my own laziness. Bad timing.

Whatever. But it wasn't due to lack of brain power or that I wasn't smart as hell. Because I was. Until...

Until in my forties when I slowly started realizing that perhaps I wasn't brilliant, or the smartest, or even smart. And now I realize I'm not only not brilliant, but I am dumb.

In my forties I started to share some "funny stories" that have happened to me in my life with some friends of mine. And my friends laughed. I enjoyed their laughter, so I would share more and more stories with them. These stories always ended up with me looking stupid. Making really dumb choices, or not being aware of the obvious, or just embarrassing myself. None of these stories made me look very good. So why would I share them? Because I thought I was confident enough that I didn't care about sharing these sort of life experiences that everyone goes through. Everyone does stupid things like this, but are too afraid to let people know. My friends would be impressed with my honesty rather than think poorly of me. Until the friend who most loved these stories let me know he has none of these kinds of experiences in his past and that what makes them so great to hear is that these happen to me consistently throughout my life. That is the moment I realized this conclusion. And giving you these stories now might just prove the point further. Why am I sharing this with anyone and everyone? My wife and kids will not be proud of me, nor will my parents. But they are stuck with me. My friends, on the other hand, will reconsider knowing me. But here I go. Enjoy.

# A Colorful
# Camp Adventure

*I* was eleven years old the first time I went to sleep-away camp. Since I was five, I went to day-camp and I never liked it, so my parents thought maybe I'd enjoy the sleep-away experience more. The truth was the only thing I liked about camp was coming home. Home where it was clean, the air was cool, and I didn't have instructional swim. At camp I was constantly sweaty and dirty, and had to sit in the sun a lot. And I was a shy kid and camp was a place for boys to yell and compete. It wasn't for me.

The idea of sending me somewhere for a month where it was twenty-four-hour camp with no air conditioning, the food was terrible, and I had to swim in a lake twice a day, wouldn't seem to be a good solution. But unfortunately for me, my parents did just that.

So, there I was at Camp Tel Sholom in Darlington, Maryland in a bunk with fourteen other boys and two counselors. Fourteen loud boys. And we'd spend our day shuffling from activity to activity. And I hated all of them:

SOCCER—I was too out of shape to be any good, and it was hot

INSTRUCTIONAL SWIM—I was scared of the water and sat on the side blowing bubbles in a bucket while the other kids were in various levels

RECREATIONAL SWIM—I could only hold on to the wall

GA-GA—This is Jewish Dodge Ball. Instead of chucking a ball at each other, we roll the ball and try to touch each other's ankles with it. Nobody gets hurt. This was kinda fun, but I always seemed to get out early.

QUIET TIME—Time to write letters or rest. This is really for the counselors to get a break. Nothing fun about it.

ARTS & CRAFTS—located in a gazebo. We had to sit on our butts on hard wood planks, but at least it was shaded.

ARCHERY—Outdoors and hot

BREAKFAST, LUNCH, DINNER—400 kids crowded in a room eating bad food

PRAYER—This was a Jewish camp so one of our activities was PRAYING?!?

RIFLERY—So many reasons to hate riflery

It is this activity at which my next story begins.

It was a weekday afternoon during the second week of my sentence, I mean of camp. Ninety-three degrees, just after eating another unidentifiable lunch. Two of my bunkmates are shooting rifles while the rest of us sit in the dirt Indian-style (my kids called this crisscross applesauce) So I'm sitting in dirt, playing with pebbles, sweating, waiting my turn when it hits me—I have to make a BM. I made BMs when I was eleven and didn't start taking shits until I was thirteen. So, a BM was soon to present itself and there were no bathrooms or even porta-potties nearby. I so hate camp. I went over and told my counselor I need to make a BM. He laughed inside, I'm sure, and then suggested I head back to our bunk. So, I did just that. I started walking in the hot sun, on a dirt path through the woods lined with brambles and thorns uphill towards our bunk. It was kind of a long walk. A couple minutes in, my walking had to slow. The turtle's head was trying to peek out. Each step was more and more difficult. I tried to physically push things back in place. Didn't help. I stopped moving for a little. I started moving again and things happened.

Actually, one very big long thing happened, and I needed to get back to the bunk quick before riflery was over and everyone came back for rest time. So, I ran with a full load the rest of the way. Once I arrived, I ran into one of the bunk's bathroom stalls, took off my pants and underpants, and cleaned myself up. I still hear no one in the bunk yet. I emerge out of the stall naked from the waist down except for my shoes and socks. I quickly throw my dirty underpants in a sink. Then I run to my trunk to find and put on a new pair of underpants, put my shorts back on. Then I go back to the sink with the intention of washing my underpants. I turn on the sink and as the water comes out, I realize I have no soap or sponge, and even if I did, I don't know how to get BM out of underpants. I shut off the sink, grab my soiled underpants and run out of the cabin, around the back where there's a dumpster and throw my underpants away. Evidence destroyed, or at least removed. For the rest of camp, I'll just put on unlaundered underpants once a week inside-out. Disgusting, but preferable to putting the dirty ones in the laundry for everyone to know what I did.

The rest of the day went normally. I was still nervous someone would see something in the dumpster but even eleven-year-old boys don't want to hang out in dumpsters. So, by the time we were all in our bunks for lights-out at 10:00 that night, I had put the day's events out of my mind and was instead thinking about how much I was dreading morning flagpole. As images of standing in the hot sun around the flagpole were in my mind, I drifted off to sleep.

"Wake the fuck up!" I didn't know what time it was, but it was pitch-black outside and my up-to-this point cool counselor was screaming and pushing us all out of our beds.

"All of you... get in the bathroom now!" We were all confused and sleepy and didn't know what was going on. This doesn't seem like some sort of camp surprise event. Not a great start to color war. So, we are all in the bathroom now and our counselor is standing in front of us and asks/yells, "Who shit green shit in the sink?"

We all peered into the sink he was standing in front of and sure enough there was a mini turd clinging to the upper edge of the bowl. And it was indeed green. And our counselor's face was a deep red. At first, I was confused and didn't think this had anything to do with me. After all it was 1:00 a.m., and I didn't fully grasp what was going on. But then it hit me. That was my mini turd. When I dropped my underpants in the sink to try to wash, and then I decided to just throw them out, I didn't think about remnants. But why was it green? I guess I was so stressed and scared, I didn't notice that my shit was a weird color. Of course, it was eating camp food for three weeks straight that did that. Runny eggs, mac and cheese, sloppy joes, and bug juice do strange things to a kid's bowels. Hence the green.

"Shitting in the sink is fucking disgusting, and whoever did this speak up now!" our counselor kept on screaming. "And clean this shit up." I didn't move a muscle. "If whoever did this doesn't admit it, none of you assholes are going back to sleep tonight and none of you assholes are going to the dance on Saturday night." The dance is a big deal at camp when the boys and girls can be together and it was a big deal to us too. But then again, do girls like boys who leave green shits in the sink? So, his threats were real and impactful. But I definitely was NOT coming forward.

I consider myself an honest person, but I didn't see any way the truth was going to set me free in this circumstance. So, I acted like all my bunkmates and stayed silent with a disgusted look on my face. My counselor hated us all at this moment. How does that make sense? This was clearly a one-man job, so why hate all of us? Unless he imagines that we all got together, and we elected one of us. We all hoisted him in the sink so he could drop a deuce. And the shit that came out was tiny and so we stuck it on the side so it wouldn't be as noticeable. And we painted it green with our extra paint from Arts & Crafts. And we planned to pridefully enjoy the look and smell of it for the remainder of camp. It brought us closer together. No. What happened is one of your campers shit his pants.

Eventually, our counselors let us go back to bed. By the next morning, the green shit was gone. I don't know who cleaned it up. The counselors from that point forward didn't like any of us and camp wasn't that fun for the last week. Everyone left camp with no solution to the mystery of the Green Shit ever coming out. And until this writing, it remained a secret for thirty-five years. What a mess.

# Pizza Delivery Boy

*I*n 1990, my parents sent me to the University of Maryland to work. By work, they meant find a major, study and work hard to become the professional I wanted to become. That is hard. So, I found easier work and spent thirty hours a week (while a full-time student) working at Davinci's Masterpizza. I started working there as a topping boy and quickly was promoted to crusts. And after a year of working "hard," I was made the assistant manager by sophomore year. This meant I not only answered calls, and made pizzas, but I also told the drivers what pizzas they were delivering to where. I was drunk with power.

Let me step back and tell you a bit about Davinci's. It was a new delivery pizza place that was just opened by the Denino brothers—Dave and Dom. They were twenty-seven and twenty-five years old and must have been miserable that they had to leave college so they opened up a pizza place in order to stay immature and drunk. The pizza was cheap and terrible. I remember our phone number was 345-FAST and when people complained that the delivery was slow and our number is bullshit, I let them know that FAST was a misprint and the real number is 345-FART. Same number, more appropriate.

Anyway, the Deninos hired a bunch of fraternity guys to be the drivers, and these guys all loved getting stoned and then driving pizza around campus. Good gig part-time for these guys. For me, it was more than a part-time job. It was an escape. My shifts were often from 5:00 p.m. to 2:00 or 3:00 a.m., and I could ignore any of the pressures I was feeling from school. And boy did I. I became the king of the operation. I learned to make the dough and sauce in the morning, I hired and fired, I did the accounting at the end of the day, I did it all. The Denino brothers were absentee owners more and more as they could rely on me.

The only thing I never did was delivery. Not once in two years, even in a pinch, had I jumped in my car with a pie, and driven to a dormitory two blocks away to deliver a pizza. First of all, I didn't own a car, but even when I borrowed my Dad's during the summer (yes, I even worked when school was out), I never did.

Until one summer day, I got a call from Dave Denino asking me to come in that night to work as a driver. Two of their drivers called in sick and since it was summer time, nobody they'd normally call was available. So, I borrowed my dad's Oldsmobile station wagon with the wood paneling, put a Davinci's Masterpizza lighted sign on the roof and started making deliveries. Deliveries were fewer and farther in the summer. Fewer because there weren't many students around for summer classes, and farther because most of the orders that came in were from College Park locals in the more residential areas. So needless to say, I wasn't making as much money and was getting lost a lot.

I wasn't loving delivery, but it wasn't terrible. For the most part I was sitting in my car or waiting at the pizza shop for the next delivery. It wasn't that hard or tiring. And I was alone most of the time and able to listen to music. It was boring, not so profitable, and I was left alone. This was just fine for me.

Around 10:00, I had just gotten back from a delivery where I got a $5 tip and was feeling really good. Average hourly income was $6 between base and tips, so $5 put me in a really good mood. As soon as I got back, Dave hands me 4 pies and sends me to Spring Hill Lakes apartments for delivery. Spring Hill Lakes. SHL. SHIT. This was an enormous apartment complex in the worst part of College Park. I knew it well because many times when I would try to send drivers out there, they would try to reject the job or claim they were out of gas and wouldn't be able to take another order for thirty minutes. It was considered a dangerous place. And I didn't want to do it, but there was no one else. So, I went.

I placed the four boxes of pizza in my backseat and started driving in the dark to SHL. Twenty minutes later, I entered the SHL complex. And this was a complex. There were at least twenty different buildings and each seemed to hide its building number on a really small, unlit sign posted on a side of the building that was obscured by trees. After driving around the complex for another few minutes, I spotted the correct building. And of course, this building wasn't one that was street side to make it easy for me. No.

I had to park in a parking lot and walk what seemed like a football field to get to the apartment door. And this was a friggin' scary walk. Nothing actually happened to me during this walk, but my mind was going crazy the entire time. It was dark. I was carrying a big, bulky bag of pizzas, and had all the tips I had earned so far that night in my pocket. And this was SHL. I was going to be mugged, or shot, or raped! I know no one was gonna rape me, but at the time I had just seen *Shawshank Redemption*, so I was terrified.

Eventually, after walking through a maze of buildings and hallways, I did arrive at the correct apartment, and knocked. A guy answered the door, took the pizza from me, gave me a $3 tip, said thanks, and shut the door... not bad. Done. Easy. Feeling foolish, I put the $3 in my pocket and start walking back to my car. As I'm backtracking my way, I look up ahead and don't think I see my car where I left it! I start sprinting now to get a closer look, and after a few more steps, I can see for sure. No car. It's been stolen. FUCK! I run back to the apartment where I delivered the pizza and told the guy what happened and asked if I could use his phone. He lets me in and shows me to his kitchen phone. I call Dave back at Davinci's.

"Dave, it's Steve. I'm here at SHL and my car's been stolen. Can you pick me up?"

He tells me he's on the way and instructs me to call 911 and report it... now."

So, I hang up with Dave and do just that. The officer tells me to wait in front of the building I'm at and he'll be there in three minutes. I'm not surprised they know where this place is and that they are close by. They probably have to come here nightly. So, I stand outside the building angry at being the victim of a theft while also being scared of being murdered by my Dad (though truthfully, I probably did him a favor by losing that wood-paneled chick-repellant).

Sure enough, three minutes later, two police cars arrive with lights on. No sirens, but the lights are definitely drawing the attention of the entire complex. As the officers exit their cars and approach me, a crowd begins to form.

So, the officers start asking me questions... what was the make and model of car, what time did I arrive, what address was I delivering to, did I see anybody suspicious, how long was I away from the car, and more. As I'm answering, my boss Dave arrives and joins me. He asks if I'm ok, and then starts cursing and complaining to the officers about this complex. He basically yells at them that they should be doing a better job. He's going a bit too far in my opinion but what do I know. One of the officers continues asking me questions as the other one leaves us to search the area. I'm thinking about calling my dad at this point and Dave is talking to all the neighbors in the crowd telling them what has happened and they should let us know anything they know. And then cop #2 returns and asks us to follow him. I guess away from the crowd. So, he leads us through a few of the buildings to the other side of the complex. As we emerge from a couple of the buildings, he points to a wood-paneled station wagon with a Davinci's Masterpizza sign on the roof. Parked nicely in a spot. The spot where I parked it. No one stole anything. As I was putting $3 tip in my pocket, I stupidly walked out the wrong side of the building. Embarrassment like I had never experienced as the police announced to everyone there that no crime had taken place. That we were all dealing with an idiot. Dave was embarrassed and pissed, and got in his car and left without saying anything to me. The police asked if I knew how to drive back (stick it to me) and then got in their cruisers and left. The crowd disappeared. I climbed into that stupid station wagon and drove back to my Dad's house. I didn't even return to Davinci's to return the pizza bag. Big Dummy.

# Becoming a Dad

*I*t's February 22, 2000. Kim and I have been married for about four years at this point, and on this morning, we are extremely excited. It is Kim's due date! She is pregnant with our first child and today is the day it is going to happen. Six months ago, Kim's doctor looked in his crystal ball and told us that our baby would emerge on 2/22. This was the date we've been dreaming of (fearing) for what seemed like eternity.

Kim was ready to get this baby out. Kim was crazy uncomfortable and on that day was larger than at any previous point in her life. Kim is a petite woman, but on this day, she looked somewhat like the girl from Willy Wonka who chews the blueberry gum... but no way is Kim floating away. I have been doing my best to keep her mind off her bodily condition, over the last month, but there aren't enough jokes in the world to make you forget that you have to fart and pee every three minutes. Kim was ready for this day for sure! And so was I. Hospital bag was packed and ready to go, and I had the list of all the people I'd need to alert as soon as it was happening. I had a full tank in the car. An extra pair of underwear for me (you never know). And the best route to the hospital set. It will happen any minute.

But wouldn't you know it, we went to bed that night and nothing happened. The doctor had lied. No baby, and Kim was still large and round. (Women love those two words about as much as men like the word TINY). We were both disappointed.

But that just means that the next day it would happen. Or not.

The next day. Nope

The next day. Uh-uh.

The next? No dice.

On the fifth day past our due date, Kim was desperate. She was nearly in tears all the time and truly thought that it wouldn't happen and she would explode. So, on that morning, I looked at her deeply and promised, "I KNOW THAT TODAY IS THE DAY. WE WILL BECOME PARENTS TODAY." Out of pure desperation, Kim believed me. Her attitude and disposition changed immediately. I had promised relief! Finally! That day she was happier than she had been the previous five. I am a great husband. But we went to bed and again, no baby.

So, the next morning she woke up even more dejected. And I looked at her again and SWORE today was the day this time. And she bought it. And again, that night, nothing.

Finally, on the next day we spoke with our doctor about the six-day-old baby that is living inside of Kim and how to evict it. It was then determined that Kim would be induced tomorrow. We weren't waiting any longer. We were taking control. We were very happy to say the least. I called Kim's and my parents and siblings and let them know that on Feb 29 we would be going to the hospital to induce labor and the baby would be born. Time to fly up here and they can be at the hospital with us during the labor. February 29, 2000—a MILLENNIAL LEAP DAY baby. Too cool.

My in-laws arrived in from Charlotte that evening and everyone was excited. The induction was scheduled for 8:00 the next morning, so that night we all stayed up talking, planning, reminiscing. We are too jacked to go to bed. But we had a big day ahead of us so at 11:30, we all went upstairs ready for the most amazing day of our lives! Kim fell asleep almost immediately. My lids wouldn't shut for another hour.

At 1:30 Kim shot up. Massive pain. A contraction. We wait for another couple contractions and realize that this baby is not waiting till 8:00 a.m. I call the doctor, wake up my in-laws, assist Kim into the car, and drive us down to Holy Cross Hospital... yes, my Jewish baby would be born under a cross. Covering all my bases? Anyway....

We get to the hospital and they immediately wheel Kim into a room that is decorated like a quaint room in your house. Nice drapes, wood floors, sofa, small table and chairs. And in the center of it all is Kim sitting in a bed hooked up to all sorts of wires and tubes and a machine beeping every thirty seconds. Doctor comes in and informs us that we aren't ready to start pushing yet and there is plenty of time before Kim is fully dilated. Time for Kim's and my family to arrive at the hospital and enjoy the wonderful day with us. At 7:00, all the family arrives. Both of our parents and my brothers and sister.

After visiting with Kim briefly in her room, they are shown to the waiting room where they must remain. And they all sat there for hours. Hours. Nothing was happening. Kim was having contractions and they hurt like hell. And I would have fun watching the monitor and letting her know when it was about to hit and how strong it would be. I enjoyed it too much. Kim was miserable. It was just she and I in this room... waiting and waiting some more.

The only interruption is when Kim's Dad would "pop in." Kim would yell at him every time, but that didn't stop his visits.

Finally, at about 4:00, the doctor announced that Kim was ready. I ran out and informed the family that the baby would be here within the hour. Everyone was excited again. I ran back in the room, and the doctor and nurses were doing stuff. Legs up, stuff in the open, and Kim is working. Push, Push, Push. Rest. Push, Push, Push. Rest. Push, Push, Push. Rest. Three hours of this! Kim was in tears, and I could see how exhausted she was. The doctor says we are going to try again and Kim says she can't.

The doctor tells her that she can do it and we are almost there. So, Kim nods her head and agrees to continue. The doctor asks me to hold one of her legs up as the nurse holds the other. So, I am seeing everything. The pushing starts again and I am waiting for my child. Nothing. Nothing is happening. Nothing is emerging. The only thing that happens is that my father-in-law screams out from behind a curtain "Push, Kim, Push!" She grabs my arm and says PLEASE DESTROY HIM. I order him back to the waiting room and then return to Kim. Pushing recommences. She turns to me and asks if I see anything? The doctor gives me a look that I understand and I say "It's happening! I see a head!" The doctor approves of my lie to my wife and encourages to push harder and harder. Kim is pushing so hard that I think the baby is going to eventually shoot out so fast and hit me in the head. But after another ten minutes we stop. Kim hates me. Vicious liar of a husband.

At this point, we are seven days overdue, and we haven't slept for thirty-seven hours. Kim's been in this hospital bed for nineteen of them, and has been pushing for three. And after all that pushing the doctor lets us know that it is time for a C-section. Surgery. I'm nervous about that. Kim is thrilled. Cut her body open and get this thing out of her. I go to the waiting room and let everyone know the new plan and remind my father-in-law to stay put. If he wants a future with his daughter or future grand-child, he will not go anywhere near the operating room. Fingers crossed that keeps him at bay.

I go back to Kim in our room, and the nurse hands me scrubs to put on. A hat, jumpsuit sort of thing and slippers that make me look like the doctor my mom always wanted me to be. They lift Kim and put her on a gurney. And we all start rolling to the operating room. As we arrive, our doctor and an assistant are washing their hands at a washing station. I don't have a clue what is going to happen. I don't know at all what to expect.

They push Kim through double doors into a very large, sterile, (metallic?) room. High ceiling. A single table in the middle of the room which they roll Kim to and lift her up onto it. They put a mini curtain across the bed by her chest. So, it is like her body is in two parts. Head and neck, and the rest of her down below. I was a tiny bit uneasy that they were going to ask me to hold her leg again, but thankfully they instructed that I was to stay up at the top by her head. And they wouldn't advise that I peek over the curtain at any time. Absolutely taking that advice. I've seen enough.

And so, it begins.... An anesthesiologist emerges from behind a curtain in the corner of the room I hadn't noticed before, and gives Kim some stuff that doesn't put her completely out but numbs everything. The doctor reminds me to stay by Kim's head. I'm ducked down by Kim's head talking to her, stroking her hair. And then the cutting begins. All sorts of sounds emanating from tools and instruments I can't imagine. The doctors are completely ignoring me right now. They are doing their work and nobody is giving me any play-by-play.

From my view, I can't see what is exactly happening at every minute, but I do observe some things. I was able to tell when they were washing parts of Kim, and then when they were cutting her, and I could tell when it looked like she was open (whatever open means). I continued stroking Kim's hair when I noticed something I totally didn't expect... a nurse was removing things from inside of Kim's body and carefully lining them up against the far wall. Bloody things I assumed were body parts that were blocking their access to my baby. I know that the body doesn't really need tonsils or an appendix, so I assumed there were other things that could be temporarily removed.

So, I went back to Kim's face and started telling her things were going great and she is amazing. Then all of a sudden, the doctor announces that our baby girl is here and he holds her above the curtain so I can take a look. I love her. She is a bloody mess. The doctor cuts the umbilical cord, cleans her up a bit, and then walks her over to an incubator that I hadn't seen on the left side of the room. They invite me to come over and meet my daughter. I leave Kim, and go over to my little girl. I stare at her in the incubator and I don't even know what is going through my mind. Life changing! It felt like a dream.

After two full minutes of standing next to my daughter, I realize that Kim's head is still stuck at the table behind a curtain, while the rest of her body is wide open. I head back to her head, and I let her know how beautiful her daughter is just like her mother. The doctors tell us that they are going to close everything up now and we'll be done shortly. So, the sounds of various instruments and tools are all around again.

After a minute, Kim asks, "What's burning?" It smelled like burning flesh.

I answered simply, "You."

Now here is where all my exhaustion, fear, stupidity, insecurity, and everything else I'm experiencing comes out in a single moment. As they are about finished closing up my wife, I remember all her organs lined up along the far wall and I still see them sitting there.

So, I stand up and ask the doctor, "Isn't she gonna need those?" and I motion to the wall.

The doctor replies "Come again?"

So, I said again, "Isn't she gonna need those things you took out of her?" and I point more directly to all of her organs. He and the other nurses look over at where I'm pointing and then turn back to me. Some smiling, one rolling his eyes, and one I can hear laughing. The doctor asks what I think those are? I'm immediately embarrassed, and although I think they are Kim's heart, kidneys, esophagus, and every other item I remember from biology, I answer "cell tissue?" What the hell is cell tissue? I don't even know what I'm saying, but no way am I saying "heart."

The doctor tries to hold in laughter and informs me that those are the rags they used during the procedure which is why they are all bloody. They line them up against the wall to make sure they are all accounted for and nothing is left inside of my wife. I know they are all thinking, "Good luck to this baby."

I go into the waiting room and announce, "It's a girl!" Celebration ensues as we all head into a new room where Kim is for the next couple hours. Then the nurse brings our daughter, Emily, to us in a bassinet and we all take turns holding her. As I am holding her, I look at Kim, and I look at Emily and I make a prayer, "Holy Cross Hospital God, please always look over these two girls all their lives. Show me how to guide them and make wise decisions. Or better yet, please put them in bubble wrap. Amen."

# One at a Time

*I*t was 2001 and my wife and I had just closed the doors on Earful of Books forever. Earful of Books is one of the stupider things I've done in my life, but there is nothing funny about it, so it isn't a chapter to itself. Merely back story. Earful of Books, or what my friend refers to as Earful of Crap, was a franchise I bought into. It was a store co-located with Blockbuster Video that rented and sold books on tape and CD. I had gotten lucky (as most people did) in the .com stock surge of 2000, but unlike most people, we sold everything before the bubble burst and put away a nice sum of money. I considered myself a financial genius! I decided to take my "hard-earned" wealth and invest it in a franchise. I read a whole bunch of books about franchising and it made a ton of sense to me.

My main goal was to buy into a franchise business that is recession-proof. A business that will survive in all economies and all circumstances and see consistent returns on my investment. So, what are those kind of businesses? Toilet-paper manufacturing, barbershops, McDonalds, day-care facilities, and more. I had looked at a bunch (maybe just a few) options and had settled on a barbershop franchise called Great Clips. It was a proven haircut business that I felt secure in. And then for some reason I gave Earful of Crap $250,000. I don't know why.

Maybe it was because they told me books on tape weren't going anywhere. Maybe it's because they told me that movie renters from Blockbuster would be dying to come rent the latest Shakespeare play at midnight. Maybe it was because I thought streaming audio was just a fad.... I don't know why I did it, but I jumped right in with no life vest. Two years later, we closed the doors and lost it all. As I said, real stupid. Not real funny.

So, my pregnant wife is holding my two-year-old daughter in her arms as she tells me, "You need to find a new career, and quick." Well-deserved pressure. I didn't know what to do or where to turn. Where I found the career I ended up in for twenty years came from this moment. I was in my accountant's office paying him $275/hour to help me with the liquidation and accounting and closing of our store/S-Corporation. Note: When I first met this CPA and opened Earful of Crap, I told this CPA that one day he'd be working only for me... (I'm such an asshole). Anyway, as he is counting my receipts from the liquidation sale (which was more money than we ever made when we were operational), he asked what I was going to do, to which I shrugged. He told me that he has a friend who manages a branch at National City and they are always looking to hire loan officers.

Keep in mind that in 2002, the refinance craze was just starting, so I had never heard of a loan officer. I asked if I would get a badge and pistol? Ends up that a loan officer is a glorified (maybe) salesman. A bank employee who sells mortgages. Works 100 percent on commission. I knew nothing about mortgages and have NEVER worked on 100 percent commission before, but my CPA's friend was willing to hire me. My wife wasn't exactly feeling like I had solved all of our problems, or even sure I was on the right path, but she loved me, and believed in me, so I took the job. I didn't actually tell her that I've never really sold anything in any of my many jobs and wasn't confident in what I was jumping into, but I became a loan officer.

That Monday I drove to National City as a loan officer for the very first time. I had a tough time sleeping the previous night and was really worried I wouldn't know what to do. But I realized that of course they would give me a couple days, or maybe weeks of training. Of course, they wouldn't expect me to just know what to do. Nope.

On arrival, I introduced myself to the secretary at the front desk and she escorted me to the manager, Ken's, office. He was the guy who interviewed me, so I was confident he'd make sure I was trained so I'd be a success.

"Hey, Steve. You make money when someone wants to get a mortgage from you. Go sell mortgages"

"How do mortgages work?" I asked. I really knew NOTHING.

"The guys can help you with anything you need. Go see Brad. Welcome to National City."

That was it. I swear nothing else. Who is Brad? I find out really quick as Brad has the office right next door to Ken and he is looking right at me standing in the hall. He asked if I was the newbie and motioned for me to come in and sit down. I do.

"This job is hard as shit. You can't do it on your own. Most people can't hack it. If you are good, you'll make almost nothing in year one. A bit more in year two. And then in year three it will all happen. If you're good. You probably aren't." Kim's gonna love this.

"Just so you know, the first guy you interviewed with didn't want to hire you and passed you on to Ken. Ken wasn't too keen on hiring you either, but I told him we need more Jews. I'm the only Jew in this branch and we need more, so I convinced him to give you a chance."

Thank you so much, Brad! Kim is going to divorce me.

"Your cubicle is by the kitchen. Go there and start reading some of the stuff I left for you on your desk. At 10:30 come to the conference room for a meeting with me and the other two top guys."

So, I leave Brad's office and try to find the cubicle he mentioned. Nobody's given me a tour of the office or anything. I don't even know where the bathroom is for when I have to throw up. I walk around this office space and quickly see that the outside window offices are all occupied by white men and the cubicles on the interior are all taken by black women. I'm not being racist... this is a fact. A weird fucking fact. I finally did find the really small cubicle near the kitchen that was mine. Clearly the other cubicles had been squeezing the walls in on this one as there was only enough room for a desk and that's about it. I almost had to climb over the desk to get in my chair.

First thing I did was call Kim to let her know that I got there and I was okay. I let her know that everyone was really nice so far and it looks like a fun place to work. After she told me she loves me (why?) I hung up. I was eager to start reading the basics of mortgage banking so I could have a prayer.

None of the stuff on my desk was about mortgages. I had information on setting up my phone, a delivery pizza menu, a company phone list, and a list of usernames and passwords... no computer on the desk, but I had passwords. I climbed back over my desk and searched for the supply closet which I found all by myself—thata boy! I got a stapler, staples, a staple remover, a pad of paper, a couple pens. A desk calendar (even though it was December), and envelopes. Why envelopes? They were in the closet.

By the time I brought my loot back to my cubicle, it was 10:25 and I had to meet Brad and the guys in the conference room in five minutes. I made the decision to leave my envelopes and staples on my desk without putting anything away and head to the conference room early. I found the conference room. It was a really long room with windows all along one side. The room was painted tan with a mahogany chair rail all along the wall. The carpet was a mixture of green and black.

Occupying most of the room was one very long, wood conference table with twenty impressive-looking chairs surrounding it. Sitting along one side was Brad and two other guys. It was obvious that I was to sit in the middle seat across the table from them. I was in an interview.

Brad started. "Steve, this is Shawn and Elliot. The three of us are the top mortgage bankers in the branch. We make a shit-ton of money. Right now, any one of us could make a call and get a $100,000 signing bonus from another bank to work for them."

What an asshole. But I believed him.

"I'm gonna make over $1M this year and they are gonna be close to that." He jerks his thumb at Shawn and Elliot. "I tell you this not to brag."

Sure.

"I tell you this because we don't want you wasting our time. We have much better things to do than spend time with someone who isn't serious about being successful. In order to be successful, you are going to need us and all the other guys here. You'll need to sit in their offices and glean what you can from their calls, you'll have to watch what they do, and ask questions. Now most of the time nobody is gonna want you in their offices. Much less bother answering your questions. They are too busy. But it is your job to convince them to invite you. There is no program to learning this business any other way."

Wow.

"And don't think you can come in here early every morning and impress us. This job is a late-day job. It means you work until seven, eight, nine, even midnight. And that usually means getting in here at around ten. So, if you come at 7:30, you are wasting your time and as a result our time."

Finally, Shawn (or maybe it was Elliot) says something. "Every single day all the LOs (I figured I was an LO) go to lunch together. Don't go on your own anywhere or meet your wife or friends. These lunches are where you will learn shit. It is where we all talk about the stuff we're working on and dealing with. We solve each other's problems. For you, this is where you are going to learn. Don't miss a lunch. We are leaving for lunch at 12:30 today. See you then."

After five seconds I realize this is my cue, so I get up to leave. Brad says one more thing.

"Get some pleats on those pants."

I want to crawl in a hole which basically I do by sitting in my cubicle.

I spend the next hour putting my envelopes away and memorizing phone extensions when somebody sticks his head in my cubicle and says it's lunchtime. I grab my keys and wallet and head to the front door where there are thirteen guys wearing solid white or blue shirts and ties. A couple are wearing jackets. Brad stands next to me (not introducing me to anyone) as we all squeeze in the elevator, walk to the parking lot, and squeeze into a few cars. I'm in the backseat of Brad's Mercedes squeezed between two other guys who were in conversation.

Now, even though it is almost winter, I am sweating like I'm at a July 4th BBQ and making the burgers. My striped (not solid) shirt is soaked and I'm very self-conscious I might smell. We get to Ledo Pizza in about ten minutes and everyone walks in the place right to the table in the back. They've been here before. It is a long table that was made by pushing four square tables together and putting a single tablecloth over it. So, everyone took a seat with Ken (the branch manager) at the head. I was left the chair right next to him. Right next to the boss. Sure.

At that point people start talking. Big talk. Loud talk. Things about their clients. Complaints about the staff (the women), company talk, commission talk. Even family talk. But not my kind of family talk where I talk about how much I love my wife, or how cute my daughter is. This is talk about how their families are there to make them seem normal when in fact they are fraternity boys hiding as professionals. All making way too much money. Years later when I saw *Boiler Room*, I felt like I had been working at J.T. Marlin... see the movie.

Surprisingly, before the waitress comes over, Brad stands up and everyone settles down. He announces that they have a new LO he'd like them to meet and points towards me. He lets everyone know that I am a good guy and am anxious to become a success as a loan officer and be a part of their team. Everybody should do their best to invite me into their offices just to let me sit there quietly and observe their routines and listen to their client calls. I won't be a pain in the ass like the last guy. (Brad knows this because, after all, I'm a Jew like him.) He then looks at me and lets me know that today lunch is on the guys. But I should be prepared to pay my share at future lunches and it doesn't matter that I'm not making the money everyone else is. Everyone pays the same. And I better have cash. A credit card fucks everything up.

I never have cash. I better get familiar with the ATM again.

All the guys are pretty welcoming to me after Brad sits down, and I perhaps feel a little relaxed for the first time that day. If you haven't picked up on it, Ken, the branch manager, stays pretty quiet and likes to let his guys train each other. He says he believes in the pressure from your peers as a motivational and teaching technique. I just think he likes not having to work.

Anyway, after we order our food (I get a salad for some reason), Ken announces that he is "Going to hit the head." This means go to the bathroom. I need to go too, so I get up as he does and I follow him to the men's room. Ken doesn't turn to me as we walk and ask how my day's going. He doesn't say any words of encouragement. He doesn't ask if I got my phone set up. He just walks.

We walk into the men's room and I stand in front of the urinal and unzip my pants and start draining my main vein. Most relaxed I've been all day.

Ken is right next to me doing the same. I keep my head straight ahead like I've always done in public bathrooms since I first learned how to use a urinal as a boy But I heard a strange sound from next to me. You see, pee on a urinal sounds like a stream hitting porcelain. Or a *whizz*. What I heard was sploshing. Like a toilet bowl rather than a urinal. I quickly steal a glance to my left to see that indeed Ken is peeing into a toilet bowl and I am peeing into a urinal. Odd. And then, it further occurs to me that there isn't a dividing wall between us as is usual in men's rooms. Usually there is a four-inch wall attached to the wall between pee-ers to give a bit of privacy, but none was present. Odder.

And then I realize with horror before I was done: THIS IS A ONE-MAN BATHROOM! My shoulder is way too close to Ken's! There are NO STALLS! I zip up my pants, briefly put my hands in the sink. And get out.

Ken is probably out of his mind wanting to fire me. At the very least he is going to tell all the guys as soon as he gets back to the table, and they will all laugh. Or even worse, he'll stay silent at lunch out of shock and then quietly individually tell the guys later about the weird as fuck LO he just hired. Either way no one was letting me in their office to "learn."

When Ken got to the table, I froze and braced for it, but he didn't say a thing. A bit of relief, but this was worse. He's really freaked out this means and will tell people later. I couldn't touch my salad. As we left, I made sure I was in the same car that Ken was in so he wouldn't tell the guys in his car. Postpone the inevitable. We made it back to the office, and I don't remember the rest of my first day at work. Nobody ever said anything to me about that occurrence... even Ken. Years later, I brought it up to Ken as a laugh and he swore he didn't remember it happening. I don't believe him. I'm such a schmo.

# Turkey Trot

*I*t's Thanksgiving Day 2011, and this year, for the first time, my wife Kim, my eleven-year-old daughter, Emily, and I are going to the Turkey Trot to participate in an annual 5K run. See, at the beginning of the year, Emily joined a team called Girls on the Run, which isn't difficult to guess what they do. Twenty girls get together every week to run. It is a great organization that promotes running, and self-confidence and sharing of experiences and feelings, girl empowerment. I'm glad Emily is part of this because in a few years I need her strong enough to fight off boys. So, I'm supportive.

So being supportive, I agree to wake up at 6:30 Thanksgiving Day and join my wife and daughter and the rest of the city on a 3.2 mile run around the local neighborhoods. I'm not a runner, but I am in decent shape, so I don't think twice about keeping up with my girls.

We drive to the race starting zone in Bethesda. We park our car on a side street and walk in the cold to the race director's desk to check-in. At check-in they handed each of us a bag full of stuff: pens, pads, squeezy things, keychains, coupons... things the sponsors desperately think we need in order to run successfully.

They also give us each a number sign that we have to pin to our backs with four safety pins. This part takes me a while, but ten minutes later, I am no longer Steve. I am now runner 03810, and proud of it.

At 8:00 the three of us go to the starting area. We were nowhere near the starting line as there were over 4,000 people racing. So, we stood in a mob of runners waiting. As everyone was waiting, they were stretching. Everyone, including Kim and Emily, had a stretch routine that they were now involved in. So, feeling left out, I joined in and mimicked whatever Emily was doing. It didn't do anything for me, but it helped pass the time until the race began. Then at 9:00 sharp, loud speakers aired a starting ring, or buzz or snap or horn or perhaps it was a British guy telling us to kindly start. All I know is it wasn't a gunshot as I had been looking forward to. At this point, the mob started moving forward. The people at the very front started racing. Those slightly behind ran, behind them people walked, and behind them the three of us moseyed towards the front. It took us about two minutes till we finally got to the starting line ourselves and started racing.

Now racing is probably too strong of a word. I was jogging at my daughter's pace. As I said, I'm not a runner and wasn't there to beat anyone or achieve a certain time. I just wanted to be with Kim and Emily and participate. Even though I'm not a runner or even jogger, as I mentioned, I'm in decent enough shape. I'd done my share of workout videos in my basement over the years and wasn't a stranger to exercise so I was confident I could "easily" keep up. I had asked Kim before the race how long a 5K or 3.2-mile race would take... an hour or five hours. I was relieved when she let me know that it would be around 35–40 minutes. Though I was confident I could run/jog for that long, I actually wasn't sure. The few times I've run in the past, my knee always starts to ache after a while, and my chest starts to hurt, and my brain tells me to stop the madness... which I usually do. So, I was a little nervous I wouldn't make it to the end. Wouldn't be able to complete a run that my eleven-year-old daughter was able to do.

So, from the moment we started running together, I was constantly thinking about how I was doing. The race took us through residential streets in familiar neighborhoods. It was really a very pretty day, just cool enough, and it was enjoyable running and looking at the changing leaves and sharing smiles with my wife and daughter. The route wasn't straight. There were route markers of where to turn and attendants at each intersection pointing in the proper direction to continue running. I was really enjoying this simple, beautiful, comfortable run with my family. But could I do this for thirty-five minutes? Did I feel a cramp? Was my chest hurting? Were my muscles giving out? Would my eleven-year-old be ashamed of a father who couldn't keep up with her? To my surprise after twenty minutes or so, I was doing just fine! I mean, this isn't amazing or anything.... Kim and Emily looked like they could run all day, but I was very relieved to realize that I would definitely be able to run for another fifteen minutes, complete the race with Emily and Kim, and then head home for some football and turkey. Perfect.

But then I started to feel a little thunder from down under. A reminder of my morning breakfast. A turtle was trying to poke his head out on this fine Thursday morn. I was in trouble. With each step I took, it was harder and harder to keep everything intact. So, after trying to continue keeping up with Emily and Kim, I slowed down to a walk. After a couple seconds, Kim realized I was no longer keeping up and turned back to ask if I was okay? I motioned for her and Emily to continue running, but Kim (understandably) wanted to know if I was okay. So, I gave her a look that I hoped clearly said, "I'm going to shit my pants. Get Emily out of here so she can still want me as her daddy and so you don't divorce me!" My look must have been perfect, because with her own look of disgust, she turned with Emily to finish the race like humans. I yelled after them, "Meet you at the car!"

So now I'm alone. And time is of the essence. Walking slowly isn't helping anything. Every slow step is still helping things proceed. Just I'm farther from the end of the race. So, I try stopping completely. I step out of the street and stand for a few seconds. Then I sit so there is a blockade pushing back against Mr. Tommy Turtle. This is kind of working. But I have no way out. I'm sitting there watching runners pass by me. A few asking if I'm okay, but ALL looking at me as they ran by. I had no solution. I could sit here forever, or I could continue running and make a mess and stink to high heaven and have to explain to my daughter at the finish line on the drive home. As I said, I was in trouble with no way out. Until I thought of something. Yes, it was a better option. Not perfect, but a better option.

I stood up and turned away from the running route, between two of the race attendants towards the neighborhood behind them. As I took a step in that direction, one of the attendants indicated I was going in the wrong direction and the race continued that way. No shit! (no pun intended). I told the guy that I had a cramp and that this was my neighborhood and I was going home. Thank God he accepted that and I started wobbling down a neighborhood street... alone... with a ticking time bomb in my pants.

The moment I thought I was far enough away from the runners, I made a 90-degree turn and went up a lawn between two houses. I didn't have a plan; I was just reacting out of desperation. I lowered my pants to my thighs, squatted next to an air conditioner unit and let nature take its course. A thick, long, solid snake emerged from my nether region, and I magically felt all better. The sweat stopped. The pain was gone. And there was no mess! As I stood to pull up my pants, I noticed I was right next to a living room window staring at a closed shade. Thank goodness for that. I could easily have had a full audience and irate neighbor. How would you react to seeing a man two inches from your living room taking a shit in your yard? Not well. So, I had to get out of there. But then my view went to the object that was beautifully coiled on the recently mowed lawn. What could I do about that? There was no leaf pile to put over it and I didn't have a bag or anything. I left it. I just ran as fast as I could to get back to the race and meet Kim and Emily at our car. As I'm running, I'm thinking that I sure do hope no one saw me. I sure do hope that no one had a security camera. But even if they did, what are the chances they'd recognize me or know how to find me? I would be fine if I could just get back in the race. And then I realize... I have a big bold number on my back: 03810—The Shitter of Bethesda. It wouldn't be hard for an irate neighbor to go to the Turkey Trot committee and ask who was number 03810. Maybe I'd be arrested? At a minimum it would be in the local papers that Steve Cohen took a dump next to someone's house on Thanksgiving Day. And if you see him doing this, please call police immediately. I am a loan officer. Which means I am in sales in the housing business. My career would be over. And Kim would divorce me and absolutely be granted full custody of Emily and Daniel. "Your honor, Steve shits in people's yards and doesn't even have the decency to clean it up. Do you really need anything further? You're right Ms. Cohen. I'm granting you full custody and a restraining order against your husband."

I ran faster than I ever have or ever dreamed I could. I got back in the race among hundreds of other people and continued running as fast as I could hoping that as people smelled a whiff, I'd be way past them. Ten minutes later I emerge from the race and spot Kim and Emily drinking Gatorade and talking with a friend of Emily's and her mother. From thirty feet away I yell, "Kim... let's go!" She grabs Emily's hand and meets me at the car. She wants to ask what happened, but I just need to get home. "I'll tell you later."

Then Emily asks, "Daddy, are you okay? What happened?" I tell her I had a stomach cramp and now we need to get home quickly so I can take medicine. She accepts this like an eleven-year-old would (I love this girl so much). We get in the car and Kim drives us home in silence. Fifteen minutes later, we pull down our driveway, and Kim pushes the button for the garage to open. I can't wait for the door's long rise, so I dart out of the car, into the garage, open the door to the family room, kick off my shoes, race upstairs, start the shower, rip my clothes off, and get in. I can't believe I made it!

Fifteen minutes later, I go downstairs, looking and smelling clean, wearing my football Jersey, wishing my in-laws a Happy Thanksgiving. I see Emily, pick her up, give her a kiss, and tell her how much I enjoyed running with her. She says, "You must have been really sweaty. You took a shower so fast!"

That night after Thanksgiving Dinner, after all the family was gone, I climbed into bed and nervously shared exactly what happened that afternoon with Kim. To my relief Kim laughed. She wasn't leaving me. I swore her to secrecy and until this writing never told another soul what happened Thanksgiving Day 2011.

But every day since then, I still check the local papers for my picture.

*The Boy Genius*

*Me and Leor in 1983 at camp. Yes, he witnessed that fateful colorful event.*

*I know how lucky I am that she doesn't leave me for something smarter..like a rock*

*Fatherhood day 1 post C-Section. God help this baby!*

*My family...I must have done something right*

Steve Cohen

*Me and my son Daniel. Friends tell me this is proof that dumbness can be passed on.*

*Kim, Emily and me pre Turkey Trot, minutes before they lost all respect for me*

*My business card when I
1st became a loan officer...
what a tool*

*Me and Dr. Friedlander...
butt buddies forever*

*The Tuesday morning Silver Diner breakfast crew.*

# Stupidity in the Workplace

*M*y first year as a loan officer was crazy. I was learning on the job during the way beginning of what was to become the greatest refi boom up to that point in history. Rates were slowly falling and every homeowner in the US wanted these lower rates. There was literally too much business for the country's loan officers to handle! This was a blessing and a curse for me. A blessing because the LOs in my office had so many leads and deals they couldn't handle and so they passed these on to me. The part of this business I was most afraid of was having to find deals. Having to bring in the business. But God said, "Let Steve Have Deals," and it was done. I didn't have to market or anything, and I was getting twenty deals a month to work on. I made money that I never thought was possible! What a blessing! But it was also a curse. I didn't know what I was doing. The staff (not the other LOs) tried to give me a crash course on getting loans through the system and that was enough to make me dangerous. I could get deals through, but things were rarely correct and caused problems for my borrowers and bank constantly. But things were closing and everyone was making money, so my business stayed this way for the first five months. Making lots of money and lots of mistakes.

Here are two of the mistakes I still think about:

I got a call from Melinda Simmons. Melinda wanted to buy a condo in Virginia. I inquired how she got my name (the referrals were starting!?) and she informed me that she called the main number and was transferred to me (how unfortunate for her). I was very happy to have a purchase loan to do and I found out the sales price was pretty high so good commission. I emailed her our application and told her the list of documents she needed to collect and fax/mail me. This was 2002 and online applications weren't yet in place, so our borrowers had to take a pen and fill out our application by hand. This application had tiny font and little room for the answers, so what came back was often illegible. Also, scanning wasn't really around then either, so borrowers had to fax their documents in. This meant that their documents were also commonly illegible. But this was the norm at the time. She promised to get these to me by the next day.

After I hung up with Melinda, I realized I was in trouble. First of all, a purchase deal meant that there would be Realtors involved. I was told that Realtors are the lifeblood of an LO's business. If they like your service, they can refer you dozens of deals annually. If they don't like you, you'll never get a referral and even worse they will let all their other Realtor friends know you suck and you'll never get ANY BUSINESS FROM ANYONE!!!! Secondly, they are buying a condo in Virginia. I have never done a deal in Virginia nor have done a condo. Both of these items required different knowledge, which I didn't have. Nervous.

The next day our office admin came into my mini-office and dropped off a fax for me (I felt important). Melinda had faxed in her application with a note that her documents would come the next day. So, could I get started? Getting started meant entering

point whenever we met. It was a surefire laugh and always started our get-togethers on the right foot.

Anyway, decades passed. Leor moved to New York and started his own family, and I stayed home and started mine. We are just as close, though we don't see each other as much. But his family still lives here, so I get to see them once in a while, which I enjoy greatly. As I said, they are my second family and hanging with them puts a smile on my face as if Leor were here. Heinan lives very close to where I live with his own family and though we don't really socialize, I do run into him often and we have become very friendly. And one time we scheduled to meet at Starbucks just to hang out. I had never done that with him before, but I looked forward to it.

The following month we met at Starbucks and had a really good time. We laughed a lot (I love Landas), we talked about our careers, kids, wives, etc. It was really nice. And we also talked about our hobbies which is when he let me know that he teaches Zumba at the gym that I belong to. Zumba is aerobics for the year 2012. I had to hold in my smile. I thought of Leor and was in danger of bursting out in laughter. But I held it together. Instead, I told him how great it is that he stays in such good shape and can even teach a class. He tells me I should take one of his classes next time I'm at the gym, and I say that I just might. Never will. But one thing I truly am is impressed with Heinan. He has always had unique qualities to him. Qualities that can make eight-year-olds laugh. But I am kind of envious that Heinan knows what he likes in life, and so just does it. Not caring what other people think. Just do what makes you happy. That takes confidence. Clearly Heinan had LOTS OF CONFIDENCE.

I don't run into Heinan for a few months when one Sunday morning, I am at my gym. I just finished doing whatever I do with the machines and free weights upstairs, and I'm toweling off my sweat walking towards the showers when I hear a familiar voice echoing over a speaker in one of the workout rooms. So, I turn towards the voice and walk over to the entrance to where it is coming from. And what do I see? Heinan Landa leading a Zumba class. Heinan is at the front of the room with a microphone thing on his head and Zumba clothes (whatever that is) on his body. And he is leading and instructing twenty women on jumps and kicks and stretches.

The room is dimly lit and the music is pumping. I watch for a minute or so when I hear, "Steve Cohen, get in here!" Heinan spotted me and waved me in. I walked up to the front and talked to him during a two-minute break. He asked if I was interested in taking this class? I told him I was and that I was really impressed with how hard it looks. No friggin way I would ever take this class, but I didn't know what to say! (Side note: I did take a class like this years later with my wife... don't tell). I asked how many classes he teaches a week and the schedule, just to continue the charade, when the class started up again and Heinan shook my hand goodbye. I walked out of the room as Gloria Gaynor's *I Will Survive* was starting. As soon as I got out, first thing I did was go around the corner, take out my cell phone and text Leor:

JUST SAW YOUR BROTHER TEACH AEROBICS
HE IS A GAY

Let me take a moment to let you know that Leor and I do not use the word GAY as an insult, or put-down, or joke... anymore. We have evolved as people and we realize how hurtful and stupid that is. I truly don't feel there is anything negative about being

GAY and using the word that way is mean, and hurtful and says more about the speaker than about who he/she thinks they are mocking.

But I didn't feel that way in the '80s and '90s. It's a fact. I use to call things gay. And Leor and I would laugh about all the things we thought were gay. His brother included (not really gay as he had a hot girlfriend). He was just... gay.

So, I sent this text to Leor to make him laugh. And I knew he would. I just used it for him and wouldn't in any other case. One problem... I texted it to Heinan. I texted it to Heinan!!!!! As soon as I hit send, I looked to make sure it went through when I noticed I sent it to the wrong Landa! Kill me!!!!!

I was still hearing his voice come through over the speakers and I wanted to die. There was nothing I could do. First of all, I just really insulted Heinan. He was going to be hurt and probably really angry and not like me very much. But secondly, just as bad, when Leor hears about my error, he would laugh his ass off louder and longer than at any time in history. And he would bring it up to me every chance he got and he'd tell everyone all the time. All I wanted to do was erase this event and never think of it again, but this was impossible. I didn't think it was funny at all. And I didn't know what to do. So, I sent a follow-up text to Heinan: JUST KIDDING MAN. GREAT 2 SEE YOU AND I'LL BE IN CLASS SOON.

Maybe he'd think I intended to send him the original text as a joke? I don't know but this was all I could think of. I went home and waited for a text response. None came that day. Or the next week or the next month or the next year. What does that mean? Was he so insulted that he was done communicating with me? Did my second text work so he didn't respond not paying much attention? Did he not use texting at all and never read it? (this would be awesome). But it was probably option #1.

I didn't bring this up to Leor for years. I figured that if Heinan never noticed it, then why poke the bear, tell Leor, who'd eagerly share the story with Heinan and make fun of me for the rest of my life. Or if Heinan was pissed at it, why have Leor refresh it in Heinan's memory?

Either way I didn't want him making fun of me for the rest of my life. I have seen and enjoyed Heinan's company many times over the last few years. At his parent's house for holidays, at family celebrations (his and mine), and have continued to bump into him once in a while round the hood. We are good and I do value my friendship with Heinan Landa. We've never talked about that text.

Years later, I did tell Leor the story hoping it was so old and I'm in the clear. When he heard it, he did laugh and laugh and laugh. We laughed like we were ten years old again. It was great. But I don't think he's ever mentioned it to Heinan. Which I'm relieved about, but I also feel bad about. If he didn't mention it to Heinan, that means that even Leor felt that my text was THAT hurtful. I still feel bad. I am more of an asshole than Leor the pinecone picking expert.

# I Hate Traffic

Okay, so it's Tuesday morning, which means I wake up at 3:30 a.m. This isn't a Tuesday thing. I always wake up at 3:30, and I have no idea why. I go downstairs, make a cup of coffee in my Keurig, turn on the local news or sports, read through my emails and texts, play Wordfeud, make more coffee and sit with my dog for three hours. Why I'm not asleep I don't know, but I cannot sleep past 3:30. Then at 6:45 I go upstairs to shit, shower, and shave to get ready to drive my son to school. We leave at 7:35 on the dot. That is my daily routine, but today's Tuesday and it's a little different. Well, it is not really different I still wake at 3:30 and I still leave at 7:35 with Daniel, but I don't go to my office after dropping him off.

I go to my weekly breakfast group at the Silver Diner. This group I started about fifteen years ago and it's basically grown to about nine of my buddies who meet every Tuesday for eggs, waffles, yogurt, or whatever, and we sit there and we talk. Talk about our wives, our kids, our jobs. Our vacations, the news, politics, credit cards. Air travel (that's a big topic that I can't stand), and laugh with and at each other. Then we all leave to work. That is definitely a highlight of my week, and I don't want to ever miss it or be late. If someone is late, which would be arriving at the diner after 8:00 sharp, then they are stuck in the seat at the very end, which means they are missing out on most of what is being talked about. Basically, missing out on the good stuff. So that is why it's beneficial to get there early enough to grab a seat right in the middle of the table.

On most Tuesdays, Daniel and I get in the car at 7:35 sharp (neither he nor I like to be late). We put on Hits1 on my Sirius Radio. This is the latest music that Daniel likes, and it helps me stay current, so this is what we always listen to. It then takes about fifteen minutes to drive Daniel to school, which makes it 7:50 by the time I say goodbye to him and he grunts goodbye to me. As soon as his door slams shut, I drive straight to the diner, which usually is about a ten-minute ride. Left on Nicholson, right on Nebel, right on Rockville Pike, and a left into the diner. That puts me in my seat at 8:00 being the third or fourth arrival. That's perfect—a few people arrive after me, and I enjoy my omelet as I hear everything that is being said from a middle seat. That is the usual Tuesday.

But on this particular Tuesday, it didn't happen that way. On this Tuesday morning, Daniel and I left at 7:35 is usual. But here is where things went off. Daniel didn't want to listen to Hits1 today. He wanted to listen to his rap music. This is what he really loved and wanted to "share" it with me on this ride. I was "cool" with it as I use to LOVE rap myself. When I was in school, LL Cool J, Kool Moe Dee, Fresh Prince, Slick Rick. These were my jams, and I was sure I'd like Daniel's jams too. But holy crap, the rap that he loved, the rap that he knew EVERY word to, was the hardest rap music I've heard. I'm talking about rap with words that I can't believe my son even knows. Racist words and words against women and words that promote violence. Words that of course teenagers would love. But it was still a shock to listen to for fifteen minutes with my son.

He not only enjoyed listening, but he knew all the words and "sang" along. I pretended to be a cool dad and bopped my head up and down. But I hated it. So, when we arrived at school at 7:50 as usual, and he got out of the car, I quickly changed the channel. Now I didn't change it to Hits1 either. I put on my favorite show... The Howard Stern Show. Now many of you know that a lot of what comes out of the Howard Stern Show is pretty similar to the lyrics in those rap songs. But it is hysterical, and so in my book that is A-OK.

On this day Howard had two of his guys doing prank calls and that is my favorite part of his show always. So, I'm driving to Silver Diner, on schedule to meet the breakfast group by 8:00 and get my prime seat. And I'm listening to Howard Stern and laughing my butt off. His guys are prank calling two Chinese restaurants and having them talk to each other, and I've never heard anything funnier in my life. As I make my usual left on Nicholson, I'm laughing to the point of tears. I'm not even aware of the driving. I'm on autopilot. Then I make my right on Nebel. All is going great. Until I can see up ahead there is a traffic jam. Cars are stopped in front of me, so I slow down and come to a complete stop. Normally I hate traffic jams, but today I was so enjoying Howard Stern and his crank calls that I barely even noticed or cared. I sat there for four to five minutes in this traffic jam listening and laughing realizing I'd be late for breakfast.

Howard went to commercial, so now I have time to start getting impatient. Then the guy in front of me, his door opens. He emerges from his car and starts walking back to me. I'm a little confused as to what he's doing. I guess that maybe he wants to use my cell phone as he is out of power, or maybe he just wants to complain to someone, or maybe he's walking to a car behind me. All I know is I turn off my radio. Sure enough he's heading to me, and so I roll down my window.

"Can I help you?" he asks.

I say, "Don't need anything, thanks."

He crunches up his face and asks, "Are you waiting here with me?"

At that point I stick my head out of my window and look down the road. I'm such a schmuck. There were no cars in front of this guy. There was no traffic jam.

He continues, "My car broke down about fifteen minutes ago and I'm waiting for AAA to get here. What are you doing?"

I could have just driven around him six minutes ago. Any normal person would have driven around him and been on their way. But not me. I decide to sit behind this broken-down car for six minutes. Six minutes this guy was probably thinking what kind of maniac just pulled up behind him. He probably has called his wife and been talking about me.

I just shot back, "Thought you might need a spotter" and rolled up my window. What the hell is a spotter?!? What did I just say? Anyway, I drove around him and drove straight to the diner. Got there at 8:10, sat in the last chair at the table. When they asked why I was late, I told them Daniel couldn't find his cell phone so we left late. At least that sounded reasonable. Blame it on my son. I'm an idiot.

# The Straw that Broke the Camel's Butt

*T*his is the story that inspired this book. I've told this story a few times to my family and friends, and I continue to ask myself why I share this. It doesn't make me look good... at all. I told this story to a few people who were in hysterics. When I told my friend Bruce this story (I tell him all my stories), he said I must put these on paper. He is my inspiration... he should be proud. I've struggled for a long time on how to write this and in fact it has been the most difficult for me to start writing. I'm nervous. Nervous I don't remember all the details, nervous I won't be able to retell the story as I have before and nervous that when I do write it down, it will no longer seem funny, but just sad. So, I've just procrastinated. I've thought about this story for months, thinking hard about how to present it comically. What words to put on paper are needed. Ultimately, I realize I don't need to do anything but tell you what happened...

Five years ago, I'm with Kim at the Silver Diner comfortably sitting in a booth eating our usual—omelet for me and club sandwich for her. We've done this many times over our marriage and I'm very good at it. All of a sudden, I start coughing a bit. And the cough continues. And it grows louder. And people start staring. My coughing fit has turned into a full-on emergency. I'm not coughing as much as choking. I'm flailing about on my side of the booth, my eyes watering, and not able to breathe. Kim casually suggests I drink some water, but I can't stop coughing enough to settle my hands or take the glass - forget being able to take an inhale. The waitstaff is slowly approaching me. People are starting to pull out their cell phones in case they need to call 911. They are doing this slowly because they assume Kim of course is going to jump out of her side of the booth and start Heimlich or mouth-to-mouth or something. Her husband seems to be dying! But she does not. Instead, she just sits there looking at her iPhone probably considering what shoes to purchase. After a full minute (which seemed like an hour), my coughing slowly subsided. I catch my breath a bit. I'm able to steady myself, I wipe away all the snot and spit around my face, and finally take a sip of water. I look at Kim, sit back, and take a bite of my omelet. Kim casually says to me, "You really should get that checked out."

Kim is not the most heartless wife in history. Far from it. She is the greatest person I've ever met and I'm grateful every day she doesn't leave me. It just so happens that this scene has taken place so many times over the past few years that Kim has become numb to it. It wasn't always that way. When this first used to happen, she'd slam my back and try to pour water down my throat. Then she'd set up appointments for me. Appointments with every kind of doctor you can think of. My general practitioner, an ENT, even a sleep apnea specialist. I've been suffering and complaining about this horrible lingering cough for years, and no one can tell what is causing it or how to help. So now I just live with it. Kim used to beg me to keep searching for a solution. But I'm tired and am done. So, Kim's no longer stressed about something I was not even willing to do anything about. Not willing to do anything about until this latest episode where on the way home, Kim demanded I mention this again to my Endocrinologist, with whom I have an appointment in seven days.

I was diagnosed as a Type-2 Diabetic about eight years ago and have been seeing an Endocrinologist, Dr. Shetty, ever since, every four months. She has become my main physician who looks at any and all health issues I have and helps me determine the best course of action... what doctors to see. I've mentioned the cough issue to her a couple times in the past but after a few attempts to fix the issue, and failure after failure, I stopped mentioning it. But next week, I will bring it up again.

Next Wednesday, I arrive at the Endocrinologist office at my scheduled time and after waiting just five minutes, I'm brought to Dr. Shetty's office (my loyalty card is full of punches, so I don't need to wait). After the cordial how's the family questions, we take my blood sugar levels, check my feet for sensation (which I have thank God), and draw my blood to test for my A1C. Usual stuff. And then Dr. Shetty asks me how my last four months have been. Any new health concerns? This is where I bring up my coughing again. I describe the incident at the Silver Diner to Dr. Shetty in detail.

She replies, "You are still coughing?!? I see that we looked into this a couple years ago. I referred you to Dr. Bosworth the ENT. What happened with him?" I respond that I don't remember and that all I know is I've been coughing, more like gagging, ever since. See, I'm exhausted and no longer hear what the doctors tell me. I see so many doctors for so many crazy things, that I can barely pay attention to what they say anymore as I have little faith they'll be able to discover what is wrong with me. So, I go through the motions and then check that off my list. And move on.

Dr. Shetty looks in her notes and sees the report from the ENT two years ago, that perhaps my epiglottis is dropping a bit, and that cauterizing it could help. But beyond that they do not see anything. Now I remember! He said that the thing that hangs in the back of my throat is longer than other peoples' (I wish that were true about other body parts), and that BURNING IT AWAY could help. COULD help! He wanted to set my throat on fire and perhaps after I recover a few weeks later, I'll have some relief. PERHAPS! BURNING! I remember I resolved to just cough the rest of my life.

But here I am again asking Dr. Shetty for help. She asks me a few more questions about the type of cough it is and determines it is time for me to visit a Pulmonologist. Check out my lungs. This make sense to me although I've always felt my breathing is clear and this is more of a choking issue. But I am hopeful that the Pulmonologist can help.

As soon as I get home, I share the details of my visit with Kim and that I have to make an appointment with a pulmonologist Dr. Shetty referred me to. Kim is so happy with this news. She tells me how proud of me she is that I finally did something about this issue and how I handled this on my own. I'm fairly insulted that she is reacting to me as if I'm one of our children... or even less able. But unfortunately, she is right to have this response. I'm pretty helpless (lazy).

Anyway, I call and make an appointment. Unfortunately, as a new patient I can't get an appointment for six weeks. So, I wait. And in fact, I completely forget about the appointment entirely until my iPhone calendar reminds me the day before.

(Warning: some of the details I'm about to share don't even make sense but whatever.)

At 10:30 the next morning I walk through the glass double doors of the doctor's office suite and on up to the receptionist's desk to sign in. Immediately I'm hit with a strange sense of familiarity like I've been here before. After signing in, I sit down and wait to be called back. As I'm in the waiting room, I'm looking around with a stronger sense of familiarity. Like I recognize the chair configuration and maybe even the art on the wall. Anyway, twenty minutes later, they call my name. I stand up and follow a nurse into the back. As we're walking back, the nurse hands me a cup and asks me to first step in the restroom and provide a sample. Huh? I'm confused why they need a urine sample? Urine isn't causing my cough. But I comply. I seem to always be giving urine samples to all sorts of doctors, so I figure since my Endocrinologist referred me, Dr. Friedlander needed urine too. Whatever. I left my filled to the line cup in the tray in the restroom and proceeded into examination room #2.

Here I waited another fifteen minutes or so until Dr. Friedlander walked in with a big smile and loudly asked, "So how can I help you?"

I recognize him. Like I've seen him before maybe. Combined with my familiarity with the office I must have seen him years ago. Maybe I did visit for this years ago and forgot. I let him know that I've been here before. At which points he looks down at his clipboard with a furrowed brow for a few seconds. He doesn't reply to that comment but looks up with another big smile, and asks, "So what's bothering you?" And so I begin:

"I have been coughing for years. It's not like a flu cough, or cold. Or congestion. It's like I'm choking. Anytime anything goes near my throat, food, water, even when I swallow saliva, I start gagging."

He looks interested. I continue:

"A couple months ago I went out to dinner with my wife and we were sitting in a booth when I started choking and the whole restaurant... I told the whole story in detail to him, even the part about how the other diners thought I have the most uncaring wife (I like that joke).

He says this sounds serious and asks if I've seen an ENT. I tell him I have, and I mention the epiglottis. He says that sounds reasonable but lets me know that he "really isn't a cough guy." I didn't know what to make of that comment. What does he mean? He's more of a wheeze guy? Or hiccups? Or whistling problems? Whatever.

He then asks me to continue. As I start again, he interrupts to ask if I could drop my pants and underwear and place my elbows on the table. So, what do I do? I quickly comply and continue:

"And the ENT suggested I cauterize the epig—WHAT THE FUCK?!?"

He just slipped his fingers up my ass! But I still continue.... And he said I could get it cauterized and that could help, but he didn't have any guarantee and I didn't want to do it. With that he removed his fingers out of my butt and again proclaimed, "I'm really not a cough guy." AGAIN! What kind of pulmonologist doesn't deal with coughs? This is nuts! But as I'm pulling my pants up, he asks me to keep them lowered and he grabs my balls. And he asks me to turn and cough.

Finally! We're dealing with coughing! Okay. So, I turn and cough as he holds my boys in his hand. And he replies "very good." But I respond no! This isn't the kind of cough I experience! He needs to hear my choking cough before he dismisses me! To which he says for the third time: I'm not really a cough guy.

As I'm pulling up my pants and zipping my fly, I look him straight in the eye and ask, "What do you mean you aren't a cough guy? What kind of guy are you?!?"

To which he smiles and says, "I'm a urologist. Why are you here?"

I'm frozen. Confused. Embarrassed. What is he talking about?

Then it hits me like a ton of bricks. Oh my God. I remember. I explain to Dr. Friedlander that Dr. Shetty had referred me to a pulmonologist to deal with my cough problem. I forgot that she had ALSO referred me to a urologist to deal with a peeing problem I've been having. I got them confused.

He was laughing his ass off. I was humiliated. His laughter calmed down enough to ask who the pulmonologist is I'm supposed to see. I realize why I got confused... the pulmonologist's name is Dr. Ball.

To which he starts hysterically laughing all over again. Through his laughter he asks me a favor. If when I go finally to see Dr. Ball and he asks me what I'm there for... I should just drop my pants. Funny guy.

It's now five years later and I've immortalized this story forever. I'm still coughing (but Dr. Ball said my lungs were clear). As for my peeing problem, three days from this writing, I'm having bladder surgery with Dr. Friedlander finally. I'm his favorite patient.

# So That's Me

*T*hese were all true stories of my life. They occurred not during a down year or period. They occurred at every age throughout. I think this means I can conclude no other way than to say that these stories are me, and indeed I am dumb.

So, what does being dumb mean? Am I too dumb to know? Too dumb to trust? Too dumb to share meaningful experiences with? Too dumb to even listen to? Yes, is the answer to each of these questions. I've concluded that this is exactly what it means.

But I also have realized that there is hope for the dumb. That dumb people can be happy. I say that because I am the happiest person I know. First of all, until I put all these stories together, I really never noticed the pattern or considered myself anything but smart and capable. So we dumb people are oblivious to our dumbness which allows us to be happy and move forward in our endeavors!

But why am I so happy? I'm not just content or fairly happy with my life. I am thrilled every single day when I wake up, and my smile usually never leaves my face. Could this be a case of dumbness to the $n^{th}$ degree that I'm not aware of all the troubles I have around me?

No. I am happy because of all the people around me. Somehow in life I have collected the very best people in the world as my family and friends. I seem to know how to maintain the best people in the universe in my world.

When I met my wife, Kim, I knew she was the very best and I proposed five months later. I've been lucky my dumbness hasn't scared her away and we've been blissful since married in 1996. Our kids have grown into two amazing, jaw-dropping people who I always want to be around. My parents, siblings, aunts, uncles, cousins... the entire family I came from, I know are the most loving and supportive and fun group of people. All these people are my family and they are part of me and I part of them. I know that they are the very best and I am happy and lucky. I may be too dumb for them, but what are they gonna do? I'm their family and they are stuck with me. Thank God.

And then there are my friends. Friends are not stuck with each other. Friends come and go all the time. Friends constantly judge and rejudge the people they are hanging out with and often opt for a change. I may have been friends with someone in elementary school who grew into better options. Someone who found me interesting at twenty-two perhaps no longer does by age twenty-three. A friend who I meet at thirty-five learns too much about me over the years and reconsiders if this relationship is worthwhile. This is the peril of us dumb people. Eventually, all of our friends will figure this out about us and we will be left alone. We are too dumb to be friends with.

But yet, that is not where I find myself. I actually have so many wonderful friends. Truly amazing group of people, who are smart, successful, loyal, giving, thoughtful, fun, inviting, and really special. And I have a lot of these people in my life and they are ALL like this. It's crazy! How have I "collected" this many exceptional people around me? It's as if I've put together a deck of cards, and the only cards in my deck are 10s, Jacks, Queens, Kings, and Aces. When I put my deck up against another deck in any game... I'll always win. In blackjack all I get is 20s and 21s. In poker, Royal Straight Flushes constantly. My friends are truly incredible.

They are so incredible that I often find myself with them and I get a bit quiet. I hear all sorts of wonderful things from them. Brilliant ideas, wonderful stories, amazing accomplishments, and impressive arguments. And I often feel I don't belong. I can't match these levels. I can't reciprocate to them, what they give to me. I'm a fraud. I'm too dumb to be friends with, and they'll catch on soon I'm sure.

But so far, they have not, and I no longer think they will. There is something about me (clearly not good sense) that attracts amazing people my way. I have no clue what it is, but there is definitely a magic element I have that counteracts dumbness. And I am so thankful for this super power. I wish I could share it with all the dumb people in the world, but I'm not sure I know how.

So, I've concluded thusly (thusly sounds smart): If my friends are all 10s, Jacks, Queens, Kings, and Aces. What am I? Merely a 4 they allow to hang out with them? No. I'm the Joker that comes with every deck of cards that you purchase. Most times, the other cards immediately throw out the joker as a waste of space in the box. But not my deck. My exemplary deck includes their joker back in the box every time they all get back in. Maybe they know there are certain games that require jokers, maybe they keep me around in case a card goes missing or rips, or maybe they just wouldn't feel like a complete deck without me.

Whatever the reason, I'm grateful. I'm happy, and I'm dumb. But not too dumb to be friends with.

Steve Cohen